YOUNG CHILDREN'S
DRAWINGS

AS A MIRROR OF DEVELOPMENT

Christhilde Blume

WECAN
WALDORF EARLY CHILDHOOD
ASSOCIATION OF NORTH AMERICA

Young Children's Drawings
as a
Mirror of Development

ISBN: 978-1-936849-49-9

Second English Edition

First published in German as Kleinkinderseichnungen – Spiegel der Entwicklung bei Gesundheit und Krankheit by J.H. Mellinger Verlag, Stuttgart.

First English Edition originally translated and published by The Attic Press, Cape Town, South Africa.

Copy Editor: Donna Lee Miele

Production Editor: Donna Lee Miele

Graphic Design: Eve Vaterlaus

Published in the United States by the Waldorf Early Childhood Association of North America, 285 Hungry Hollow Road, Spring Valley, NY 10977

www.waldorfearlychildhood.org

Visit our online store at store.waldorfearlychildhood.org

This publication is made possible through a grant from the Waldorf Curriculum Fund.

TABLE OF CONTENTS

Author's Note

During the Second World War, Michaela Strauss was left thousands of children's drawings by her father, the late Hanns Strauss (1883-1946), one of the earliest Waldorf teachers. She went through them systematically and noticed that certain drawn shapes were linked to a specific age and stage of development.

Her studies convinced her that these stages were not confined to European children, but could be seen in drawings from all over the world. This finding confirms statements made by Rudolf Steiner in his many lectures on child development.

Michaela Strauss's observations encouraged me to start collecting drawings and paintings in my own pediatric surgery, and these present-day pictures show the same characteristic as did those from the nineteen-thirties. I concluded that they express the developmental milestones each of us undergoes in early childhood. Steiner's observations on the development of the human being offer a key to the puzzles with which these drawings confront us. In *Education of the Child in the Light of Anthroposophy*, he describes in detail the development of the physical body and its integration with the soul and the gradually incarnating human spirit.[1]

The process by which the soul and spirit gradually "work through" the physical body as they make their way into it, as well as the growth of individual consciousness, are experienced by the small child, and are expressed in the pictures he or she draws. The adult learns to "read" from these pictures what the child has to say about his or her inner self on the physical, psychological, and spiritual levels.

It is the aim of this study to draw the attention of parents, caregivers, and educators to these drawings, which can provide insight into the amazing process during which the soul and spirit come to terms with their co-existence in the physical body, as these processes are mirrored in images we can learn to read and follow.

I wish to express my sincerest thanks to Michaela Strauss, whose book *Understanding Children's Drawings* appeared in 1977. I owe to her the impulse to find a new way of studying the development of the child and of following up the difficulties children experience as they find their way into life. I also thank those parents who have collected their children's drawings and shared them with me.

I wish to express my heartfelt thanks to all the friends in Germany and South Africa who helped to make this English edition possible.

– Christhilde ßlume

INTRODUCTION

Children's drawings are a source of infinite fascination. As we gaze in wonder at what children draw, we long for a key to understand what is happening within the child that these drawings reflect. The research by Michaela Strauss, which looked at over a thousand children's drawings from earliest scribbles up to school-readiness person-house-tree compositions, resulted in the Waldorf classic, *Understanding Children's Drawings.*[2] This study observed that predictable archetypal forms and patterns follow a consistent sequence corresponding to typical chronological and developmental ages. Other researchers in the mainstream reflect similar findings. Children all over the world use the same expressions in their drawings—no matter what the geography, race, or cultural orientation. In other words, drawings of children all over the world reflect their path of incarnation into the physical body.

Michaela Strauss' book was first published in 1978. In 2004, Audrey McAllen's *Reading Children's Drawings – The Person, House, and Tree Motifs*[3] expanded the look at how these three elements can develop in form and elaboration over time. With Dr. Christhilde Blume's *Young Children's Drawings as a Mirror of Development*, published in English in 2000, we have another exciting guide to explore the path of children's visual language.

Dr. Blume begins with a clear and concise summary of Michaela Strauss' overview of the progression of forms in drawings, from little tykes' first swirling, circling scribbles and linear crosses to the appearance of closed circles, spirals and squares, onto triangles, and explains when these appear in drawings. She relates these to the threefold faculties of thinking, feeling, and willing and to the progression of activity of the fourfold physical, etheric, and astral bodies, and I-being of the child. Her writing is notable for its clarity and accessibility and is worth our reading for this presentation alone.

What is a new contribution to this study is her sharing of how drawings change when a child works through an illness with strong fever. Rudolf Steiner emphasized again and again that a strong warmth process assists the I-being of the child to incarnate into and individualize the physical body. This process is supported through soul warmth, warmth of interest, engendered warmth of physical activity, and engendered warmth of fever, to name a few. Many of the illnesses Dr. Blume describes are obviously much less common today, but they provide important examples of how children express and experience their individualization. Dr. Blume's observations invite us to recognize and support healthy warmth processes, on all levels, as a guiding companion on the path to incarnation.

1.
HOW DO SMALL CHILDREN DRAW?

Figure 1

Let us take a look at the scribbles, drawings and paintings a small child normally creates up to his or her seventh year. We notice that the forms and "symbols" in drawings made by children of more or less the same age are very similar to one another, whatever culture or race these children may belong to. From the time the child is able to pick up a pencil, a crayon or a ballpoint up to about the third year, circular sequences appear on any surface that may be available, and they appear at lightning speed. No explanation is given. They simply curve into existence. When there is a range of colors to choose from, frequently the sequence begins with light colors such as yellow or orange (heavenly consciousness) and proceeds in ever-darker whirls of lines, progressing from red to blue and even into black (approaching earthly consciousness).

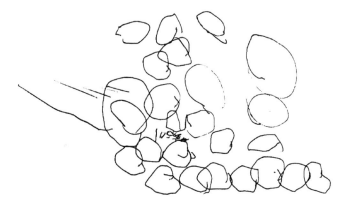

Figure 2

Gradually, this hasty circling movement comes to rest in a single circle which can be "closed" if the child so wishes.

Figure 3

At the same time another form swings into visibility: lines cross. This theme is elaborated at a later stage.

Where both these formative tendencies combine (circle and line), the human being is represented for the first time.

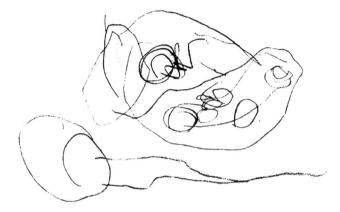

Figure 4

After all, it is the human being itself to which the small child turns for orientation. In rising to an upright position by sitting and standing, the child imitates those around him. From the start, the small child patterns himself on the adult's thoughts, emotions and actions.

Between the third and the fifth year of life other symbols can also be "read" from children's drawings. As the child works at expressing a human figure, circles and squares are now interrelated in rhythmic sequences. So far, the child has lived in the forces that create the circle. The square puts in a kind of preliminary appearance where lines cross. In these interconnections of forms definite shapes, such as faces, appear. The body is no longer represented only by lines. It is given a specific form, such as the oval, the ladder and similar motifs.

Figure 5

Figure 6

Increasingly, the child perceives the world around him in greater detail. Between ages three and four, children attempt to express people, animals, trees and houses in the forms of their drawings. When we ask what these indicate, the same forms may be given a variety of names on different occasions.

Indeed, the children may express amazement when we ask them such questions, which seem superfluous to them. At four, the children draw themselves in the surroundings, from which they look out at the world around them.

Figure 7

Figure 8

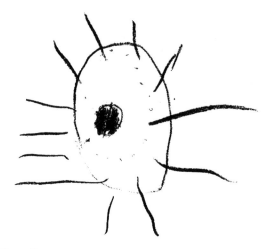

Figure 9

In doing so, they try to connect with the world with feeler-like lines.

Figure 10

Figure 11

At age five, they draw themselves looking out into the world from the house, from some sort of enveloping place. They can also draw themselves standing beside these surroundings, looking both at the world and at themselves.

Figure 12

Children paint or draw the life situation they are in. The spiral, too, appears as a theme in their world of forms, as in the center of Figure 12.

Figure 13

Between the fifth and seventh years a new shape appears in children's drawings: the triangle. It appears in everything the children draw at this stage, whether they are houses, people, or anything else (see "Further Steps" in Chapter 4).

Figure 14

Up to this time the drawings have had a linear character. Now the pictures show blocks of color and take on the character of paintings, even if they are still drawn with colored crayons. Perspective does not as yet play a part .

The drawings and pictures we have examined so far allow us to "read" the process of human development from the time the child picks up a pencil to the age of seven. The spirit and soul take hold of the physical body step by step. In doing so, they awaken individual consciousness in distinct stages. The spirit-soul organism makes its way to incarnation from its home in the spiritual world into the material world of physical substance. It enters into earthly conditions from out of the cosmos which had completely enveloped it. This is a path taken not only by each individual human being but by mankind as a whole. From the sleeping infant, as yet entirely unconscious of the earthly world, this path leads to the dreamy relationship with the surroundings which characterizes the small child, and reaches the gradual process of knowing where one stands, experienced by the awakening boy or girl of seven. Three distinct stages of consciousness can be observed, and these are reflected in the drawings and pictures children produce.

From the time when young children begin to draw up to their third year, the circle is the dominant form; this is followed by the square and the spiral during the next two years. Between the ages of five and seven, the triangle begins to appear. All these shapes, however, always relate to the interpretation of the human form.

How can we learn to understand the relationship of these shapes to the stages of consciousness in child development? A few basic facts need to be established.

2.
THE HUMAN ORGANISM: A THREEFOLD SYSTEM

The human form is built up of head, trunk and limbs. Within the body, a still clearer system of threefold organization can be seen in the way the functions of the organs are interrelated. The head, and inside it the brain, is the seat of the quiet center of the nerve-sense system. The brain matures in three distinct stages during the first years of life, up to the age of nine.

The upper trunk encloses the rhythmic organs of heart and lungs. These are gradually attuned to one another during the development processes of childhood.

The metabolic organs are embedded in the lower part of the trunk. These organs are in continuous activity as they carry out the processes connected with digestion and bodily movement. Their restlessness presents a strong contrast to the resting head, which is carried calmly on the neck and shoulders.

The threefold nature of the human form is related to specific tasks performed by each of the three integrated systems housed in the body. The round form of the head is an image of the starry heavens in their majesty, an image of the cosmos. In the bony skull the brain, enclosed and motionless, is the physical basis of an activity performed in a state of wakefulness: thinking.

In the curved, horizontal cage of the ribs, the upper trunk encloses the rhythmic system with its representative organs, the heart and lungs. The ribs spring outward from the vertical spine to form the chest in beautiful symmetry. Heart and lungs are the physical basis of a second stage of consciousness: that of feeling.

The consciousness in our feelings has a lower degree of wakefulness than that needed for thinking. It is more closely akin to our dreaming consciousness, somewhere between sleeping and being awake.

When we have a shock, "our breath stops," or our heart can "jump for joy." Such expressions show how deeply the rhythmic system is linked to the life of the feelings, and how we are made aware of our feelings by changes of rhythm. The human being's relationship to the world around him is expressed through sympathy and antipathy. Goethe has expressed the experience of this middle rhythmic sphere in the human being in a poem:

> There are two kinds of grace in the taking of breath:
> Drawing in the air, and releasing it again;
> The latter oppresses, the former refreshes;
> So wonderfully is life mixed.
> Thank God when he presses down upon you,
> And thank him when he releases you again.[4]

The lower part of the trunk, where the metabolism and the limbs are centered, provides the basis for a third state of consciousness: the will. In expressing the will in practical activity, the human being moves his limbs, thus activating the metabolic system with its continuous organic processes of destruction, construction and transformation. In comparison with the awakened state of consciousness in the head, this state of will-consciousness can be compared with the dimmed consciousness of sleep. Our waking day consciousness has no access to it. We are not consciously aware of how our limbs move, or of how our digestive system functions.

The forms of the bodily organs relate to the archetypal shapes found in the children's drawings:

- In the upper part of the human being we find the rounded form of the skull that is reflected by the child when he first starts to draw a circle.

- In the middle there are the spine, ribs, heart and lungs (the cross, spiral and square).

- In the lower region we find the bones of the limbs, radial in character (straight lines in the child's drawing), and the bowels as a cross-section (triangle).

- In the realm of the soul, a threefold character can be seen in the activities of thinking, feeling and willing, that are linked to the three integrated systems in the physical body. In these activities three states of consciousness, each with varying degrees of clarity of consciousness, correspond to the actual conditions of waking, dreaming and sleeping.

We can sum up and say: The human being stands before us with his rounded head containing the brain, which is the basis for waking, conscious thinking: with his chest, in which heart and lungs are rhythmically active, in a dreamy state, forming the basis of consciousness for feeling; and with the lower part of the trunk and the limbs, dealing with the processes of metabolism and forming the basis of the will activity, which operates in a sleeping state of consciousness.

Into this threefold human being the individual spirit and soul organism gradually incarnates in a series of stages. Let us examine these developmental steps in order to understand what is going on with a greater degree of precision.

3.
THE FOUR SHEATHS
OF THE HUMAN BEING

The physical body forms the first sheath encompassing the human being. It is the densest component of the human being: we can touch, hold, measure, and weigh the physical body. In bones, teeth, sinews, and so on, it contains the solid substance supporting us. This substance has a solid shape which is subject to the laws of physics. Examining its consistency, we see that the physical body is immovable, firm and lifeless. The solid element is also found in nature, outside the human being. The mineral world consists of this substance. Minerals carry the same laws of form in themselves and are similar to the solid, supporting substance that is our physical body.

The liquid element within the human body is entirely different: a watery, streaming quality is found in our blood, in the lymphatic system, in cellular liquids and in the fluid around the brain. The etheric body is the invisible entity that works with and in these fluids, and can be regarded as the "fluid human being." This etheric body forms a second sheath. It cannot be perceived by the outer senses. However, all of us can observe the effect of it at work, in the soil, in plants and animals, and in humans. It is a bearer of life. The etheric body makes use of the liquid element in order to do its work. Without the streaming, living quality of liquid, everything that is now alive would cease to live. Life itself would be annihilated. In the physical structure of the plant, we find the etheric at work in the circulation of sap. The living plant world permeates the physical earth with life.

A further element comes to work in the human being through the air and all its effects. We read that God breathed the breath of life into Adam, who then became a living soul. It is as a living soul that we can experience joy and pain, desire and disgust, elation and depression within ourselves—in short, everything in the way of feelings and concepts that come and go within us. In this airy being of man, which is connected to the soul, the third sheath of the human being works. Spiritual science speaks of it as the astral body. Within the astral body we can distinguish thinking, feeling, and willing as activities of the soul. We experience each of them with a specific degree of consciousness. In this aspect of the warm-blooded soul, animals and humans are related to one another.

The fourth sheath of our being makes us truly human beings, as distinguished from animals. It is that element which enables us to perceive ourselves as individuals. It is only human beings who can refer to themselves as "I," or "myself." Ancient myths, such as the Greek tale of Prometheus, describe how a spark of fire radiates within us as the I, the ego. The element of fire, of warmth, lives and works in the human being as the ego.

Human beings require a constant body temperature (warmth) in order to maintain their specific level of consciousness. In states of fever or at subnormal temperatures, this level of consciousness cannot be maintained. A constant temperature is not only required for the state of awakeness in which we function during the day. It must also be held during the night, despite the fact that the ego is in a different relationship to the other elements of the human being when we sleep, compared with waking.

If the body cools down during sleep, we wake up—we grow aware of our body temperature and must wrap up and return to normal warmth.

Animals have a different relationship to body temperature. Each species has its own particular state of temperature, depending on the way it relates to its environment. This temperature can be fixed at different levels from one season to the next. Differences between human and animal temperatures can even be observed in the embryo.

Let us examine the four sheaths of the human being in relation to the four elements (minerals, liquid, air, warmth) and to the realms of nature.

- Within our physical body we can find the solid, earthly substance of the mineral world.

- In our etheric body we have the streaming liquids, which we find in the plants.

- In our astral body there is air, enlivening the soul in both animals and human beings.

- Our ego exists in the element of warmth. As a spark of light and warmth within us, it raises the human being above the realms of mineral, plant and animal, and is the essence of his or her humanity.

Although the ego, the astral body, and the etheric body are not visible, their effects can be observed in everyday life.

4.

THE DEVELOPMENT OF THE CHILD IN THE FIRST SEVEN YEARS OF LIFE

Introduction

We have seen that the human being is both of a threefold and a fourfold nature. In the course of observing a child's development in the light of both these aspects, we shall find it easier to understand the drawings that are produced during the first seven years of childhood.

Rudolf Steiner has characterized the infant and the young child as functioning as "wholly sense organ."[5] What does this mean? A sense organ (the eye, ear, tongue, skin, and so on) mediates between the human body and its surrounding world. Impressions of all the realms of nature—stones, plants, and animals—enter into the child, as well as the thoughts, emotions, and actions of human beings. It is as if the whole child becomes imbued with the impressions that come to meet him or her. The souls and spirits of children seem to be like a floating sheath around them; they are not yet able to reflect on an inner world. In the infant and the small child, everything that streams toward and into them makes an impression and affects them right down to the formation of bodily organs.

Sense organs are also a gateway to the world, and through them, human beings perceive their surroundings. Perception goes out from the child through the gates of the senses. It is, however, an activity that is impossible for the infant.

A very young child still lives within its own world and will have to sense its way into the outer world. When we are born, our parents give us our inherited physical body, which is a kind of model for us to work with. The other three sheaths (etheric body, astral body, and ego) which during pregnancy surrounded the embryo from the outside, begin to work their way into the child, thereby transforming the physical body step by step.

After birth the child remains within the protection of the mother's warmth of soul. Together with all those concerned with rearing the child, the mother needs to try to shape the environment so that the three sheaths can work upon and mold the child in the best possible way.

In the first seven years of life, the etheric body draws into the physical body and transforms it. It is through this gradual transformation that the constitution of the individual develops. This occurs in three great stages: from birth to the third year, from three to five, and from five to about seven years old.

The Development of the Child in the First Seven Years of Life

As the infant develops, the first thing that shows is his or her gradual awakening into the gesture of meaningful movement. At first, limb movement is uncoordinated, but gradually a kind of order develops. First, the head is raised, then one sees the child grow aware of the movement of her own hands by looking at them. After learning to sit, towards the end of the first year, she has taken hold of the muscular system to such a degree that she can begin to stand and then to walk. The ordering ability living in the head permeates the muscular system, and within the first year, limb movements become harmonious and then give way to the rhythmic activity of walking.

A second impulse sets in during the following year, in which the child learns how to speak. The child now discovers that everything has a name of its own. In acquiring words, the child gets to know the world. In learning to speak, within the realm of the air, the astral body's impulse streams towards the child from the astral sheath which still surrounds it. It is also grasped at by the child within.

Through a third impulse, at about three years, the child begins to use the word "I" when referring to herself. Again, we see one of the sheaths still enfolding the child being grasped at from within. The experience of being an individual lights up within the soul. This is indeed an experience of light. It is an impulse from the ego itself: I am me, myself, I am an "I." In connection with this experience, the first germinal attempts at thinking come about.

So we see that in the child's development from infancy, it first grasps hold of the will through the limbs by beginning to walk, then takes hold of the middle area, which has its life in the airy element and helps her to learn to speak. Finally, the child makes use of the nervous substance, thus enabling the first processes of thought to take place.

In the first three years we can see two streams of development moving in opposite directions: physical maturation moves downwards from head to toe, and the development of the conscious abilities of walking, speaking, and thinking moves upward. Taking control of one's own body is related to the faculty of orienting oneself in space.

These phenomena that we observe during the first three years of a child's life can help us understand rhythms of greater magnitude that are repeated in general maturation throughout our lives. In the first three years we seem to see an early image of what can come to fruition in later stages of life. What develops at an early stage can be regarded as a germ of things to come.

In the drawings of a three-year-old, we see the moment of development in which the impulsive circling of the early drawings are left behind. A way inward is now found to the "circle" (see Figures 2 and 15).

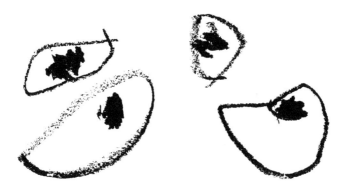

Figure 15

These drawings show development toward the child's early experience of the ego in its germinal form, which will only reach maturity at age twenty-one. The circle that has been drawn is an unconscious image of the round skull. The consciousness of the small child remains in a world of its own, in the sphere of the will. As observers, how do we become aware of this?

We all know the delight of young children running round in circles or in curves, with their arms raised, almost unable to stop. This movement expresses the fact that the sleeping world of the limbs and the metabolism is unconsciously "perceived" by the opposite pole of the head activity. At this point of development the child is still entirely embedded in the experiences of his body. Movement itself has become a pleasure to be enjoyed. Life gives one pleasure, pain is felt when illness is on its way, and in short steps the child learns to know how it relates to the three-dimensional space surrounding it. The child as a being is still engaged in imitating the cosmos.

From Infancy to Childhood

During subsequent developmental steps, up to about the fifth year, further changes take place. The child becomes more aware of feelings and emotions living in the will, and of thinking, after the movement of the will has been enjoyed. Here, heart and lungs do their work in rhythmic form. The bloodstream takes the carbon dioxide from the body to the heart, and takes oxygen from the lungs to the heart, where both streams are caught up in vortices (spiral forms) and flow away again, back into the body and into the lungs.

The main area of the child's experience has thus moved away from the pole of the metabolism and its liquid, eternally moving activity. It has passed to the rhythmic area within him that is most closely related to the air. Sleeping dreams—like the consciousness of the child under three—now give way to the dreaming sleep of feeling. This characterizes the next two years. In the group experience of kindergarten to which children can now be exposed, they meet their new playmates in group games, and in playing with friends become increasingly aware of the world around them. Now children are not so closely bound to the experience of their own bodies as they were previously. They are exploring new possibilities and discovering the world in various ways.

Tasting, smelling, seeing, and the experiences of heat and cold open up new gates of perception, and they are experienced with increasing confidence. In painting, modeling and singing, and in other forms of informal art work, as well as in listening to fairy stories or in dressing up for all sorts of imaginative play situations, forces are called upon which grow within the hearts of the children. What is sown here can become the seed for the future. It can later enable the human being to rediscover those spiritual realities that, in bygone times, were experienced as a matter of course.

Along with the whirling bloodstream, the heart is the organ connected to the streaming and liquid metabolic system. With its rhythmic activity, the heart belongs to the middle region, but in its action of creating vortices, it is related to the lower pole in the human being. Now the child begins to live more strongly in his feeling realm, although in a dreaming fashion.

The lungs are the other organ of the rhythmic human being, and they draw our attention in the opposite direction. They point to what we have called "the upper human being."

From this upper human being the etheric, formative forces arise, and the tendency to density and stability enters. The moment a child is born, his or her lungs take in a first breath of air, and so the child is actively engaged in connecting with the world.

Between their third·and fifth years, children refine and strengthen their relation to the earth by means of the senses. They are then in a state of consciousness which is connected with dreamy feelings. Both the heart and lungs are positioned in the upper thorax, enclosed by the spinal column from behind and the rib cage at the sides and in front. It is in this intermediate realm where the streams of development from above and below encounter one another. At this stage, the etheric body enters the middle realm and works on the rhythmic organs in the much the same way as it did in the first three years on the head. In the relationship between the heartbeat and the breaths taken every minute, distinct steps of incarnation can be observed.

The process of gradual adjustment between the upper and lower poles can also be regarded as a struggle between the formative forces and those of vitality. We can "read" the way this struggle proceeds if we look attentively at the children's drawings during this time. There are spirals, like the vortices in the heart (see Figures 12, 16, 17).

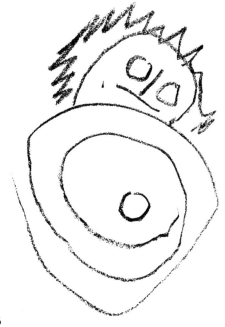

Figure 16

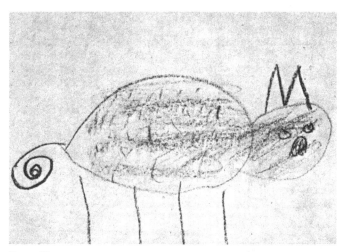

Figure 17

There are trees like the spine, ribs with the heavy trunk, and the branches, whose forms are repeated several times, leading up to the crown of the tree (Figures 5, 18).

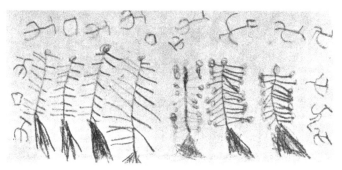

Figure 18

The ladder with its right angles and the square of the house—these are indeed images of the lungs and the chest (Figures 19, 20).

Figure 19

Figure 20

The life-giving bloodstream from below turns into a vortex and encounters the stabilizing tendency in the nervous system from above in the cross: life and death are facing one another.

The teeth, made of the hardest substance in the human body, are represented in symbols reminiscent of fences (Figure 21). Around the fourth year of a child's life the milk teeth have matured, and at the same time they begin to make way for what are to be the permanent teeth of later life.

Figure 21

A further image of what is happening within the child's development can be seen in the frequent drawings at this stage of a head with legs, and sometimes also arms and hands, attached to it (Figures 9, 10). These show the head, which has already emerged from its sheath as a circle, surrounded by the "limbs" appearing rather like feelers. On the one hand the circle that the child developed in the first three years appears, and on the other, we see the "feelers" which represent the new-found awareness in sensing the outer world (Figure 22).

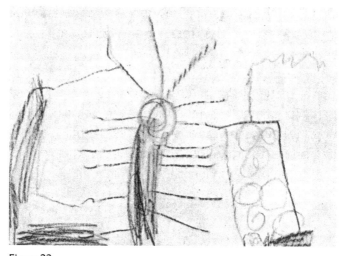

Figure 22

We can see the child becoming more independent. There is a great deal that children now want to do on their own, and the word "no" is never very far away. The being of the child has emerged a little further from its protective sheath. The child is now able not only to look outwards to the world, but is beginning to establish his own inner world by feeling the first steps in separation from the surrounding world (Figures 11, 23).

Figure 23

Further Steps

In the following phase of life, between the fifth and the seventh year, the streams of development gradually go their separate ways. They can be observed by looking in two directions.

The stream of the etheric body that is striving downwards now begins to mold the limbs and metabolic system. It takes hold of the child's body, transforming it from the "model" to the personal physical body of the individuality. Such renewed will activity not merely brings about the joy of learning to stand and walk, which we saw during the first year of life, but also enjoyment in acquiring new abilities with hands and feet. Roller skates and stilts come into their own, as do scooters and bicycles. The desire to do every-thing oneself seems to grow day by day, and the children are keen to help adults in what they are doing. There is a new awareness of one's own body after the fifth year has begun. In engaging with and taking initiatives in the surrounding world, the child is strengthening his own will. We, as parents and teachers, need to create an environment worthy of imitation.

Rising up from below, the second stream reaches the head. There are now new possibilities of meeting and getting in touch with the world outside. To the child, the world seems transformed, as new access to it is gained. A gradual awakening of the ability to think can come about through the maturation of the nervous substance. Listening becomes a more intentional activity, the thought content of the spoken word is grasped, and people around us are recognized as human beings, like ourselves. It is not games in bigger groups—such as the ring and singing games enjoyed between the third and the fifth year—which the children now want. Characters or little scenes from stories they have heard take hold of their imaginations, and they dress up purposely to suit the part rather than simply adapting to whatever costume happens to come their way. Connections form between individual children or between definite groups. The child's soul now begins to emerge from its own world. It opens to the world around it in ever-widening circles. The activity of thinking is now on its way, but logical conclusions such as those the adult makes are not yet in sight. This can be seen in the following example: At mother's birthday, there are three short candles and one tall one on the birthday table. A five-year-old enters, sees the candles and says: "You are four and I am five." The mother asks: "But is Mommy younger than you are?" The answer is utterly clear and convinced: "No!" Of course the mother is the older of the two.

The style of drawing also undergoes a change at this point. In colored pictures, a new form comes to the fore: the triangle. It makes its appearance in human figures, in the roofs of houses, and so on, quite naturally (Figures 13, 14, 24, 25).

Figure 24

Figure 25

Now the child sits down to draw something definite, something he has remembered or imagined, something from a story or something that occurred in daily life. We can now be told what it is that the drawing represents (Figures 26, 27, 28).

What does the appearance of the triangle tell us about the development of the child? It is a symbol of light, used throughout the ages in art as a holy sign. It is concealed within the metabolic and limb system in two places. The child has shaped and formed its physical body, starting from the head and moving downwards. Now, between ages five and seven, it is concerned with transforming the lower pole of limbs and metabolism from the "model" the parents have offered. As we have seen, this is done by means of the etheric body. It is in this lower area where the will is centered.

Figure 26

Figure 27

Figure 28

When the etheric body penetrates the will and metabolism, the child expresses it by introducing a triangular shape in the drawings, the symbol of light. Thus we see how in a cross-section of the colon one finds an inverted triangle, and likewise in the womb, indicating a holy place on earth. An inner situation is expressed by an outer form. The same thing holds true for the "sun wheel" or "steering-wheel" drawn by five-year-olds (Figures 29, 30).

Figure 29

What can we guess at from these phenomena? In the development of mankind there was a period of time in which perception took place in a dreamy state of consciousness by means of the sympathetic nervous system, the solar plexus. This is positioned near the stomach and has become a rudimentary organ, having been replaced by the central nervous system.

Figure 30

We have seen the way the child passes through various stages of consciousness in the course of development. At five, children stand on the verge of their dreaming, half-awake consciousness on the level of feeling and are on the point of entering the thinking, waking consciousness. This form of consciousness is centered in what we have called "the upper human being." At the same time, the etheric body is at work in the metabolic and limb system in the stream of development which runs downwards from the head. It is in this system that organic transformation is now taking place. During this process, memories of an earlier stage of human development are dimly experienced.

Tremendous vistas into the development of humankind and of the individual human being, as well as the relationship of the one to the other, can open for us if we only grasp what children's drawings tell us at this juncture.

In the seventh year, at the end of this phase of life, the process of densification and transformation has been completed to such a degree that the child's first physical metamorphosis can be seen: the spine has now developed the necessary curvature, from being much straighter as a baby; the shoulders have leveled out, the waist is formed, the baby pot-belly vanishes, and the first molars appear as permanent teeth. Their function in preparing food for digestion indicates their relationship to the metabolic system, that pole which the child has just made his own. The etheric forces previously involved in transforming the physical body are now partially free of this task and can take on the new activities needed for memory work and thinking.

The child is now ready to enter school, because the freed etheric forces can now proceed to give form and shape to thinking. In the following two periods of seven years the physical body will be worked on, first by the astral body and then by the ego. Up till this point they have been working on the sheaths of the human being from outside, as it were. A description of this process would go far beyond the present scope of this book.

Summary

Let us now review the development of human beings during the first seven years of life.

The first insubstantial image of the rounded form of cosmic spheres grows into dense substance as the spherical skull. At the end of the first period, up to the third year, a first experience of the ego flashes up. The infant can still be regarded entirely as a sense organ attempting to grasp the world by imitation. The movements of organic maturation processes stream downward through the child from the head. By its transformative activity, the etheric body works on the "model" body handed down by the parents, enabling it to become the instrument for the elements of soul and spirit which stream inwards and upwards from below. In these developmental processes there are certain critical points, within the threefold organism of each child.

In the upper being, we find the round form of the skull, caught in images drawn by the child as a circle. The cosmic element manifests in the realm of the physical. In the middle area of the human being, we find the chest, caught by the child in images of the spiral (representing the heart) and the square (representing the lung), where a new beginning for further development appears. Here, the densification of earthly form takes place, and what the child is aware of in this process appears in the drawings as a square. In the lower area of the human body we see the metabolism reflected in the child's drawings by the form of the triangle as a symbol of light, representing the spirit enfolded in the physical body.

During the first seven years, the child learns to know the world by means of imitation. Working inwards from without in the course of this activity, it relives the incarnation of the human being. After being enfolded in the warmth of the cosmic realm, we gradually grow into the density and stability of the physical. Humankind's path is one of finding the ego within oneself. The outset of the journey lies in the cosmos, in the warmth of divine powers. This warmth is drawn into the human being during this process.

These events are reflected right in the processes of the body. In the formation of blood, the direction from outside to inside can be traced. Blood has its start in the warming layers of tissue that surround the embryo, and then gradually finds its place in the marrow of the bones via the organs of heart, spleen and liver. In running round and round in circles, the small child imitates this awe-inspiring cosmic process.

Thus the completion of the first stage of development is reached in the seventh year. After being "wholly sense organ" at the beginning of his earthly journey, the child is now able to use the basic senses to serve him, passing through in either direction, inward or outward. The etheric body has been freed for the activity of thought, and active perception of the environment opens new vistas and possibilities for the child.

After learning by imitation, the preschool child has now become ready for school. Over and above the ability to learn by imitation, children are open to the guidance they will meet in the world of adults, a guidance which is about to play a formative part in the next seven years. Learning from teachers and educators, the children further develop their soul abilities of thinking, feeling and willing, enabling them to move into the future.

5.
CHILDHOOD DISEASES

The first part of this book presented the development of the child as a path generally valid for each one of us. Every individual reflects the whole development of humankind during the first seven years of life. Traces of this development were pointed out in the symbols and drawings that children create as they grow up from infancy. Children show what they experience unconsciously as their bodies are being transformed. They need help to go through all these stages of development and to overcome obstacles in transforming what they have brought or inherited, and turn them into part of themselves. Woven into our destinies are aids to develop and reinforce this. They are known as childhood diseases.

Here we are dealing with sicknesses which put in a "physiological" appearance during childhood. They arrive when there is an "inner situation," a readiness or disposition to pass through a more or less dramatic process in the course of going through the stages of development. Here we include scarlet fever, mumps, measles, whooping cough, chicken pox and German measles. When adults have to go through these sicknesses, they become more violently ill and may be in greater danger than a child is, due to the fact that the process is being undergone at a different age and in a completely different phase of personal and physiological development.

How do childhood sicknesses take their course?

Here are some case histories.

The temperature of a child rises to fever heat, there is a violent cough, the nose is running, the eyes are sensitive to light and have begun to water intensely. The face looks bloated, and after several days a spotty red rash appears on the face and on the head. The spots soon start expanding over the whole body into red areas which run into one another. We can see that the child has caught measles. What can these symptoms tell us? We realize that the watery element has got the upper hand; the child is bloated and "wet"—everything seems to be "runny."[6]

Another child is not running a high temperature. The tonsils are inflamed and show white spots of pus. The patient vomits and a rash appears, gradually spreading upwards from below in tiny pinpoint-sized red spots that seem to cover the skin. If we pass our hand over the skin it feels warm and dry as velvet. This child is "dry" and "hardened," suffering from scarlet fever.

Yet another child has a mild fever, not very high, but the patient's cheeks feel painful, and below one or both ears, large, soft swellings arise from the parotid glands, spreading to the throat and the lower parts of the cheeks. The countenance can be compared to a hamster's; the child is suffering from mumps. If we want to find an expression for the symbolic character of this sickness, we will have to imagine the enlarged gland behind the ear, the parotis. Everything glandular in the human body is deeply related to the balance of liquids in the entire body. Any swelling will point to a superfluity of liquid in the organism.

A different set of symptoms arises when a child begins to cough without any particular trouble for about ten days to a fortnight. If the cough increases in violence, at night more than during the day; if in addition the coughing comes and goes in powerful attacks and the air is drawn in spasmodically; if finally the child throws up thick and ropy white phlegm, then we are faced with a child who has caught whooping cough. This sickness points to the struggles between too much form (spasms) and an energetic resistance to this tendency (coughing up phlegm).

Childhood diseases and child development

All these forms of sickness show two sides of the human being. One of them points to hyperactivity of the formative forces (dryness, vomiting, spasms), the other shows us that the watery element is gaining too great a prevalence (bloated appearance, excess moisture, swollen glands, coughing up phlegm). This draws our attention either "upward" or "downward" in regard to the human being.

At the upper end of the body where the brain rests inside the skull, nervous substance offers the "mirroring activity" by means of which we think. We are awake when we are active in this way. The brain's shape is based on symmetry. It is formed and drawn out into a closely meshed web of thread-like structures. In ever more delicately spun filaments, the nervous system, centered in the skull, extends the nerves into the entire body, right into the skin at the uttermost periphery. It offers us an image of the formative process that streams downwards from above. As is the case with the mineral world, the nerves lack practically any regenerative potential. When people stay awake for too long, they tire and feel utterly exhausted, and salt deposits (mineral substance) can be traced in their brains.

Lungs as well as the brain have the tendency to be affected by formative forces, despite the fact that the lungs are themselves an organ of the "airy organism" of the human being. This airy organism works on the rest of the body, exerting a certain amount of pressure on it when a breath of air is drawn in. The air forms us and then releases us again.

The aim of the metabolic system, on the other hand, is to build up the body as a whole. But this activity is concealed from consciousness, as though the human being were in a deep sleep in this sphere. Both the upper nervous system and lower metabolic system work on the whole of the organism. There is a process of destruction, originating in the upper pole, and one of building and rebuilding originating in the lower. We breathe in and out in the middle realm, and we become conscious or unconscious when waking or sleeping. In observing these states of being, we can watch one or the other of these centers of forces at work. They come into play alternately in a physiological way.

Sickness is a state in which either of these two polarities outweighs the other in its effect on the body and soul of the human being. When the formative forces and thought activity prevail, the upper human being and the airy organism get the upper hand. We may be faced with drying out, with vomiting or spasms. We can see an effect of what we have called the astral body or the soul of the human being: the soul is closely linked to the ego, our own personal being inside ourselves.

When the regenerative forces become too strong, form is lost, substance appears to overpower all that was previously shaped, and we are faced with a child that seems to be predominantly water, with a bloated body. These effects come from a one-sided working of the lower pole of the human being. Here we can observe the effect of the etheric body or life body and everything related to it. It is more directly oriented towards the physical body.

In childhood sicknesses, children attempt to deal with the struggle between elements tending towards supporting form and those tending to overcome it. It is a struggle, as it were, between air and water.

In chickenpox such a conflict with the watery element actually takes place. There is a rash of small red spots; in the center of each a watery blister forms. This soon bursts and forms a crust. In German measles, there is a red rash of larger or smaller extent, the glands swell, and the temperature rarely rises. As in mumps, we must look to the watery component inside the human being.

What do all these childhood diseases have in common? There is a rash spreading all over the skin. What does this say about the condition of the child? Particularly during the first years of their lives, when the children are primarily "sense organs," they react to what comes to meet them with their entire being. The skin reflects the state of our inner lives and our bodily organs. It encloses the human form in its personal, individual shape. It can help us to understand the struggle that goes on during childhood sicknesses. At birth, it is not only the "model body" offered by our parents that is turned into something bearing our very own constitution, but also part of their own "watery" and soul conditions. It is through the children's diseases that all we have inherited is transformed into our own unique being.

What force is it that comes to help the child overcome a one-sided condition? This force is known as fever.

Fever

Fever is a holistic process taking hold of the entire being of a person, a process produced by the human organism itself. The metabolic activity is heightened and the temperature rises. The process going on within the metabolism calls forth an answer in the head: the individual's ego strength moves down to overcome the onesidedness of the sickness and leads the individual to a new and healthy state. One must remember that it is only at a temperature of 103°F (39.5°C) or more that a virus can be overcome. The process of regaining health is such that it always offers a new starting point for further development.

How do we know? After recovery, we can observe the child. We listen to what the parents tell us, find out about any new abilities they have noticed, and look at the children's drawings. In most cases, children who have gone through children's diseases show an increased stability, and difficulties on many levels that had previously seemed insurmountable now suddenly seem to find their own solutions. The children are often more harmonious, more radiant and find renewed joy in life; on the other hand, a new level of seriousness and purposefulness seems to have been reached. A step in the inner development of the individual has been taken.

A number of examples may serve to show what can be observed in all children's sicknesses.

Figure 31, Figure 32 . 2½ years. Before and after measles

Figure 33, Figure 34. 2 years. ßefore and after measles.

The children represented in Figures 31-34 have not yet reached the stage of calling themselves "I." They are still entirely enclosed in their "sheaths" and have only just begun to work upon transforming their "model bodies." This is obvious in the drawings. The children are not yet in a position to go through an inner step of development. The drawings do not show much change before and after sickness.

Figure 35, Figure 36." 2½ years. Before and after whooping cough

Figure 37, Figure 38. 4½ years. ßefore and during whooping cough.

Figures 35-39 show the developmental steps the two children have taken. The symbolism has changed during the sickness. The human figures that had previously been represented quite simply can now be seen clearly and distinctly, almost radiantly

Figure 39. 4½ years. After whooping cough.

After going through the sickness, the child who drew Figure 39 has emerged from his or her own world. There is a house to look out of. The child can regard him- or herself from the outside.

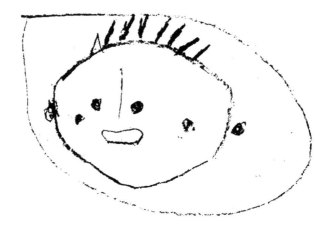

Figure 40, Figure 41. 4½ years. Before and after whooping cough.

After going through the sickness, the child who drew
Figures 40 and 41 has emerged from his or her own world.
There is a house to look out of. The child can regard him-
or herself from the outside.

Figure 42, Figure 43. 4 years. Before and after measles.

Figure 43 of the Three Kings dates from after the illness. Does it not poignantly express how the previous way of experiencing the world has been transformed?

Figure 44, Figure 45. 6½ years. Before and after measles.

As a "late developer," the child represented by Figures 44 and 45 has transformed a chaos of colors into a well-ordered drawing, showing she is almost ready for school.

Figure 46, Figure 47. 6 years. Before and after whooping cough.

From expressing an infantile image of the human form (still closely bound to a symbolic representation) before the onset of whooping cough, the child who drew Figures 46 and 47 has now found her way to drawing her subject in such a way that feelings of striving and joy can be seen in the gesture of the human figure.

Figure 48, Figure 49." 2½ years. Before and after fever.

The same process of taking a step in development can be seen after a fever. After a feverish sickness, areas of color in Figures 48 and 49 covering parts of the paper are succeeded by the figure of a human being groping for its environment, seeming to send out antennae to find it.

Figure 50

Figure 51

In the course of a fortnight, a 4 1/2-year-old child had several attacks of fever reaching up to 104°F (40°C). There were hardly any other symptoms of sickness. Every day a new drawing was produced. Figures 50-53 clearly indicate the inner struggle for development. Here we can only give a selection. What was chaos at the onset of the sickness gradually becomes a well-formed picture of three people with a house, a tree and nature all around.

Figure 52

Figure 53

Figure 54, Figure 55. 3½ years. Before and after pneumonia.

Before her attack of pneumonia, the child who drew Figures 54 and 55 had never touched a crayon except to produce tiny dots like those shown above. After her illness, this "late developer" began to draw the circles usual for her age, but already closed them firmly, pointing to an ego experience that could be noticed in her development.

Figure 56

In cases where it is possible to allow an illness to run its course, it can also bring about an inner development, if treated homeopathically and not simply suppressed.

This step in development can also be observed beyond the first seven years, in school and elsewhere.

Let us give an example: A girl aged seven years and ten months had been sent to school too early. Despite all her efforts and the help offered by the adults, she could not cope with her new situation, so that she was finally sent back to kindergarten. Figure 56 dates from that period. The sky is dark, the tree seems to have had its upper branches lopped off.

Then the child caught whooping cough, and after that she seemed to have been changed into a new person. She couldn't wait to go back to primary school, she was perfectly able to follow the lessons, and finally drew Figure 57–this

Figure 57

time a light-filled, harmonious drawing, with trees that were beautifully shaped.

Here, we must stress an important distinction we have to make in evaluating the drawings: in the first seven years of life, it is the symbolism which is central. We look at the symbolic forms underlying the objects represented in this or that drawing (e.g. circle, square, triangle, spiral, ladder). These symbolic forms are alike for children of the same age-group all over the world. We are dealing with the inner development typical of all children, everywhere.

In the following seven years of life, this symbolism fades away, to be replaced by an individual way of representing what one has seen, remembered or imagined. The individual soul gets to work on its own "model body," and transforms it for the use of that particular personality. Now we have to come to grips with the personality of the child who has drawn the picture: his or her human identity, character, temperament.

Summary and further outlook

Summarizing what we have considered so far, we can now understand that a child who has undergone a childhood sickness—or any other serious state of illness—benefits from the experience. This is because the child's inner development generally takes a step forward. A question now arises for the doctor who accompanied the child as a patient throughout the period of sickness, doing so in such a way that the sickness was not cut short by medication.

This question is whether it is justified to simply break off an ongoing process of development by suppressing the disease. What are we actually doing when we stop the course of an illness? What are we doing when we prevent the onset of a sickness by inoculation, or if we decrease its effects—or if we alleviate the fever by means of lowering the temperature?

Are we permitted to stand in the way of an individuality making its way into life? Shouldn't a doctor rather try to further and support this development where possible, to watch carefully over the course the sickness takes and try to protect the development of the personality?

I conclude with the wish that my attempt to point out these steps of development before and after childhood sicknesses will help to promote confidence in the development processes in children. May it alleviate, or even set aside, the anxiety which is produced from all sides in our time so that the path may be freed for the development of the child and for the fulfillment of his or her task on earth—which is the right of every human being.

CHAPTER NOTES

Author's Note

1. Rudolf Steiner, *The Education of the Child in the Light of Anthroposophy* (GA 34). See, e.g., Rudolf Steiner, *The Education of the Child* (Great Barrington, Massachusetts: SteinerBooks, 1996).

Introduction

2. Michaela Strauss, *Understanding Children's Drawings* (Revised Edition, Forest Row, United Kingdom: Rudolf Steiner Press 2008).

3. Audrey McAllen, *Reading Children's Drawings – The Person, House, and Tree Motifs* (Fair Oaks, California: Rudolf Steiner College Press 2004).

Chapter 2

4. Johann Wolfgang von Goethe, "*Talismans.*" Translation from The Attic Press. See, e.g., *Goethe's Reineke Fox, West-Eastern Divan, and Achilleid* (London: G. Bell & Sons, 1890) at 203 for a published translation.

Chapter 4

5. See, e.g., Rudolf Steiner, *The Kingdom of Childhood*, Lecture 2 (Great Barrington, Massachusetts: SteinerBooks 1995).

Chapter 5

6. Note to the First English Edition: In South Africa, measles is a serious illness.

CPSIA information can be obtained
at www.ICGtesting.com
Printed in the USA
FFHW010650310519
52749961-58272FF